ACROSS tHE TRacKS

ACROSS tHE TRaCKS

Copyright © 2016 by Brooks, Dennis L., Rockdale, Texas

All rights reserved under the Pan-American and International Copyright conventions

Printed in the United States of America

ISBN:978-0-9968711-1-2

Library of Congress Control Number

All rights reserved. This book may not be reproduced in whole or part, in any form or by any means, electronic or mechanical, including photocopying, recording, or by any information storage and retrieval system now known or hereafter invented, without the permission of the author.

Unless otherwise indicated, Scriptures are taken from the King James Version. Copyright© 1979, 1980, 1982, Thomas Nelson, Inc., Publishers

Across the Tracks

Draped in Praise Publishing, LLC., Hammond, Louisiana

Draped in Praise
P O Box 1106
Hammond, LA 70401
www.drapedinpraise.org

Across the Tracks

And they shall build the old wastes,
they shall raise up the former desolations,
and they shall repair the waste cities,
the desolations of many generations.
Isaiah 61:4

Across the Tracks

Dennis L. Brooks, Sr. PhD

###############################

Preface
###########

This is to provide history of Rockdale, Texas, on the east side of town, the place I call home. The place that I left for many years. After I established a career, married and had a family, I returned home with a vision to make a difference in my community. A change that will make a difference for generations to come.

This book deals with the account of the town from a black perspective, my perspective. It shows the obstacles faced and what blacks went through to not only survive, but to thrive and make life better for many generations to come.

This is not to criticize any nationality, religion or way of life, but to reveal how life has changed over several decades. It is also meant to bring awareness to those that might be going through hard times, unemployment, lack of vision, lack of purpose and not truly understanding God's purpose for life. My prayer is that the history of Rockdale will not die, nor will it ever repeat itself. As we come together, embrace our differences, and understand that we all have a purpose, then we can see how every person has a role to play in this life. How you love others and yourself is a testament to Who God really is in your life.

Dr. Dennis L. Brooks

Acknowledgements

I give thanks to the Lord for saving me, filling me with the Holy Ghost, empowering me to impart and pen this book with the help and support of my wonderful wife who has been my helpmeet for 53 years. We have stood together and have seen God do wonderful things in our lives, even when we did not represent Him wonderfully. Clara is a part of every page, because not only did we experience some of the same things growing up, but we also grew up in the same city, went to the same school, and experienced some of the same ups and downs.

This book has been in the making for 10 years, I got the encouragement from my wife to take the time and finish it, however, the Lord had to send the little woman at the well, (Debbie McNair-Allen) one of our Seminary students to also encourage me to finish as well as publish this book. Thank you, Debbie for listening to God.

I also thank my community for being a part of my growing up, because if it were not for you, there would be no story to tell.

Dennis L. Brooks, Sr. PhD

Foreword

##########

Spoken words from Ms. Susie Sansom-Piper at Sho'Nuff Restaurant for Heritage Day in Rockdale, TX. Ms. Piper is the oldest living teacher that taught at Aycock school, where Dr. Dennis Brooks was one of her students. Here are some words spoken by Ms. Piper on April 22, 2016:

My, my, my!!! Where Sho'Nuff sits is hallow ground. This place and where the church sits is the ceiling of long ago. I remember the stories and from my own memory of the shops in Rockdale. Rockdale was established in 1824, and it was called a railroad town. The train passed through twice a day. It was later known as the town of Black Gold, Midnight Coal. It is now a city museum with many facts of life. It has increased with people who have bigger goals and more elaborate dreams.

I remember talk about the slave houses, and I saw some as well. Blacks lived everywhere in Rockdale. But across the tracks had some different living conditions, not all bad, just different. There are still some vintage homes in Rockdale and some of the living conditions have not all been upgraded. Yet one thing that I can say about Rockdale: we never had the massive riots or events that others endured during segregation. There were no fights, nor hatred that kept us from loving each other. We had our differences. We quietly integrated. Rockdale did not keep love out of the community. We were friendly. We would pat one another on the back, and we always helped each other. We had the best schools, with the smartest children, who have grown to become teachers, nurses, city officials, coaches, and other leaders throughout the states.

Rockdale offered a lot to our future generations. I am happy that I made an impact on so many students, but really the students made my life. Dennis Brooks, (I had a nickname for him, but I will leave that out), was one of my greatest students. He now is running a church, owns a restaurant, and provides instruction and teaching for students at his seminary school, which sets in the spot where he attended school.

As you enjoy this writing and review you own life, I say to you – write yourself! Answer these questions and start to change the course of history for your life and generations to come.

- Who am I?
- What do I want to do with my life?
- Why am I doing it?
- When do I do it?
- Where will I do it?
- How will it affect my life and others?

Once you answer these questions and live out your life with passion and integrity. All I can say is MISSION ACCOMPLISHED!

Spoken words by Ms. Susie Sansom-Piper
Heritage Day at Sho'Nuff Restaurant 4/22/2016
Aycock School & Rockdale Teacher

Dennis L. Brooks, Sr. PhD

Table of Contents
##########

Preface 6

Acknowledgements.. 7

Foreword 8

Introduction 12

Chapter 1: The Meaning of Across the Tracks 16

Chapter 2: The Time of Segregation 22

Chapter 3: The Infrastructure – Community Appearance... 26

Chapter 4: People in the Community 34

Chapter 5: Business in the Community.......................... 42

Chapter 6: Church Life in the Community...................... 48

Chapter 7: Social Life in the Community........................ 58

Chapter 8: Work Life in the Community......................... 64

Chapter 9: School Life in the Community....................... 70

Chapter 10: The 1950's Change –Large Company Shift.... 76

Chapter 11: Now – The Transition and Transformation...... 80

The Challenge... 90

About the Author 92

Across the Tracks

Introduction

############

As the youngest of four children, I was 13 years younger than my sister. We were more than a decade different. An entire generation of changes set us apart.

I was born and raised in Rockdale, Texas. I was raised by both parents. My dad was a man of short stature. He was about five feet two inches tall. Yet he stood as though he was more than six feet. He never backed down from anyone or anything. My mother was about five feet five inches. Her entire family was tall. My twin uncles were very close to six feet three, and my oldest uncle was about six feet, with a weight of about 300 pounds plus. My mom was sharp and very intelligent, yet she had a submissive spirit about her.

During my time of growing up, there were not many divorces, or we did not hear of it. People stayed married and did all they could to keep family together. My parents were affluent in comparison to many of the blacks during my time of growing up. In my younger years, we were called colored, and there have been many other names given to blacks. Some of the names have been very derogatory, based on a feeling of inferiority rather than the color of our skin or our nationality. Whatever the name, we are who we are by the grace of God.

Across the Tracks

My dad's grandmother was a native African. She spoke the original African language. My mother was what they call a Malatto – mixed breed of black and white. I am sure there is some Indian within the bloodline, but during my time of growing up, you were either black or white. You were a part of the have or have not. You were rich or po'.

I grew up in Rockdale. Graduated high school in 1960. Amazing to note that the Institute that now houses the seminary and workshops is on the site where I started school, as a child. I grew up on the Eastside of town which was called Grass Burr Hill, and I lived on 6th Street.

As I reminisce on times past, you can have a sense of what happened and how transition took place to change the small town and other rural towns nearby. As you read, you can also see that some change did take place, but it took a long time to take effect on the town as a whole. It wasn't until the last decade that some major changes were really noticeable. I am a true testament of how change has occurred throughout history, and how God can bring about change in life, if you choose to accept what He has to offer.

Dennis L. Brooks, Sr. PhD

Across the Tracks

Chapter 1
##########

The Meaning of the Tracks

Every small southern town had an area called "across the tracks." You could hear the sound of a train approaching or leaving at any time of the day or night. Across the tracks was known to people or those who was not black, as a place "not" to go. It was considered dark, down, and dirty. When you left the town to come across the tracks, there was a dip in the road and things went from elevation to depression, both physically and mentally. There were no street lights, pave streets or street signs. There was no running water or indoor facilities. The housing was very much substandard. There was electric on the inside, but outside, when night would fall, you couldn't see your hands before your face. It was a place of doom. A place that could keep you down, deep in depression and despair. It was said by one of the oldest citizens, "that the eastside town was used as a dump ground." This was before more Blacks moved to the east side.

My family was a semi-middle class family, because my father worked for a millionaire. We had a well in our yard. Mostly everyone on the eastside had a well in the yard. Our home was descent compared to some of the others. Some lived in substandard houses, but they were always clean. Some homes had holes in the walls and the roof, most homes had tin roofs. There was no insulation back then to keep the heat or the cold in. So when it was hot, it was hot. We would open windows or some would have fans to cool off the house. When it was cold, it was sho' nuff cold. On a rainy day, it was nothing for the roof to leak, because of the holes in the tin roofs.

We did not have running water in our homes. There was no inside plumbing. Our toilet was outside, even though the house I grew up in was built by the agricultural department. Some had the capability to purchase water by the barrel in the city for five cents per barrel, a truck was needed to haul it to the house.

But for us (those who were black), it was a sanctuary. It was a safe place. It was home. It was a place to be. It was where things happened. When everyone around you is poor, you do not know you are poor. This is all you see; it was a way of life. It is hard to see better when you are confined only to what you know and see.

The roads we traveled were made of dirt. We did not have the luxury of black top roads or asphalt, which were noted when you left the eastside of the community. We had dirt roads. We did not seem to mind the dirt roads. Well, we did not mind until it rained. A portion of across the track was red-clay dirt. This was plentiful on the hill where I lived. Going from the hill to flats was sand. Sand that was deep. Sand that people would get stuck driving wagons pulled by horses. I know you know the difference in red clay dirt and sand, but for the younger generation reading this, red clay dirt was fine dirt that lacked any gravel or rock. When it was mixed with water, it would become like a paste, depending on the amount of water mixed with it. When it dried, it became hard and compressed like concrete. Compared to sand, which has fine grains of rock, it did not have any consistency of forming any shape. The more water mixed with it, the less stability or traction when weight was applied. So when it rained, the rain would wash out the roads immobilizing passage of those who had cars. It would hinder the white people as they came in the **day time** to pick up workers. I emphasize day time because as young people, we had made a pact. If we caught any whites across the track at night, we would "get them." We planned to turn their truck over and beat them up. Then we would run. Now before you shake your head or pass judgment, we did not hurt anyone, nor did we cause harm. They did the same things to us, if we were caught downtown or on the west side after dark. It doesn't mean it was right, but during that time of my life, we thought it was fun, while it was also a way of survival.

There were other small towns nearby that had similar events and shared some of Rockdale characteristics. They were Taylor, Hearne, Cameron, Rosebud, and Giddings, just to name a few. The tracks are still in place, and some things are still the same; very little has changed. The tracks in town, whether railroad tracks or the tracks of family and growing up, have left memories as a track that continue to hold many captive. The tracks of the past can hinder some from moving forward in life. The tracks of family history and familiarity have paralyzed some from tapping into the potential and purpose of what God has in store. I will refocus and stay on track (excuse the pun) with what the original intent of this book is to convey. As a child, I had fun growing up. But as I am looking back on it, it was hell!

Dennis L. Brooks, Sr. PhD

Across the Tracks

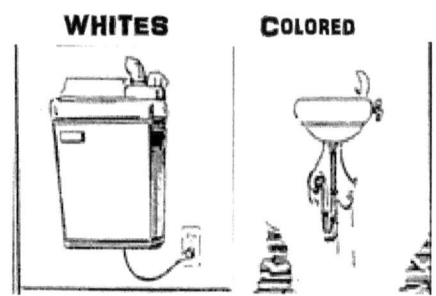

(picture taken from blacklikemoi.com & altered)

Chapter 2
##########

The Time of Segregation

I grew up in times when things were black and white. There was no in between. Everything was separate. The schools were separate. The churches were separate. The public restrooms were separate (if there were any for blacks at all). The water fountains were separate, and the community was separate.

When it came to businesses, blacks were not allowed to dine in or sit in the same areas to eat with whites in any of the restaurants. Blacks were only allowed through the back door to the kitchen area where blacks were employed. They were the dishwashers and cooks. When it came to eating at a restaurant, blacks had to order from a separate window for food or depending on the establishment, they were only allowed to go to the back and order.

There was no public transportation in the city. We had to walk everywhere we went. Very few people, where I lived, had a car. There was a passenger train that came through town. A train that stopped in town was a sign of industry and life, as well as a future for potential prosperity. The train had separate cars for blacks and whites. The last car was usually reserved for the colored. They were not allowed to eat or dine on the train. They had to bring their own food and usually it was carried in a shoe box or brown paper bag.

Across the Tracks

When we attended school, our books were used books and were very late additions that came from the white school system. The books were as much as 10 years behind on information. We had no way of obtaining up-to-date literature. However, our teachers were brilliant in teaching us how to make the best of what we had. We definitely received a well-rounded education despite challenges, when we graduated we were prepared for higher learning institutions, there was no excuse not to have a good foundation of education.

Segregation was a way of life throughout the United States. I was not aware of all the events and news that transpired because we did not have television. We had no way of knowing what happened, unless someone physically came in town to spread the news. I guess we lived by the cliché of "no news is good news." I had no idea about all of the things that transpired in the south, until I left home. It was later in life that I heard and witnessed all the horrific events that took place in America – the land of the free! Events such as what happened with the march in Selma, the lynchings in Mississippi, the bombing in Alabama in the Sunday School class, and other things that people turned blind eye and deaf ear to segregation and racism. I truly thought it was just a way of life in Rockdale. The Bible is correct, as we are reminded through one of Paul's letters when he stated that your brothers and sisters are going through the same things.

Now, I know better. I pastor a church with all nationalities, backgrounds, and cultures. I am a believer that we are all equal. God has no respect of person. He uses whom He pleases. He is faithful and just to forgive our sin. He reigns on the just, as well as the unjust. His favor is not fair, but He is just, and He is faithful.

Across the Tracks

Chapter 3
##########

The Infrastructure – Community Appearance

Infrastructure is important in the foundation of building. Whether it is a physical house or managing your life, your foundation will determine how strong you are when storms arise. Rockdale was no different than any other town when it came to infrastructure. The town's infrastructure or foundation included a legal system, places for shopping, schools, multiple businesses, a post office, churches, medical care, houses and many community activities. The differences were similar, but unique in comparison to across the tracks. There were three entry points across the tracks that led to the neighborhood where I lived. The entry at the ice house was thriving and seems to have better life conditions, until you got across the tracks.

Every community has its strong characteristics, as well as its weak points. There is a reason businesses were located on Main Street. Main Street is the thoroughfare for all traffic, be it residents, visitors, or passer-byers. Across the tracks is totally different. Across the tracks is a community all within itself that stands apart from the city. When you traveled across the tracks near the Ice House, it seemed as though you were leaving a place elevated high above your expectations or where you believed dreams would come true, only to enter another part of a community that seemed to be destined for doom and gloom. Still in the same city, but a change like night and day. As you crossed the tracks, there was a decline, and the road went from smooth, well-manicured asphalt or tar, to rough gravel or dirt terrain. As I recollect the process of riding across the tracks, the vision was a dreadful memory of lack and loss of hope. Oh, don't get me wrong, we had life across the tracks. We were just existing, not truly living and definitely not living abundantly.

There were several sections in our area. As you ventured into the neighborhood, depending on which side of the tracks you entered, you encountered the initial section that had houses made of wood that were not always attached to a secure foundation. They were sometimes elevated on blocks. There was a section of the area called "The Flat." The Flat was kind of the bad section of the neighborhood. It wasn't bad because of major killings like today, but there was a group of boys or men that would start fights with other blacks in another area of town on the other side of the tracks. I guess in today's time it would be called a gang, but we considered them sort of the poorest of the poor. Yet across the other side of the tracks was a black community called "The Bad Bottom." It was called the "Bad Bottom" because of a group of men that always was prepared to fight and ran those gang members back to the Flats. They would sometimes get run back to their area in defeat, yet it never stopped them from standing their grounds and defending their turf. I do not remember much roughness of "The Flats," as I think of this with a smile, but there were others who knew of things that I did not always see. When you lived in

"The Flats," you sho' nuff did some living. "The Flats" was where many people hung out.

Our homes were not jammed close together like apartments. There was plenty of space to spread out and grow. The houses were built by men that had skills, but were not licensed in construction work. They learned skills from working on farms and repairing for the whites. It was a skill or trade handed down from previous generations, but there was no recollection of certification or licensure. Most probably could not afford it financially. But they did what they had to do to ensure the families had a roof over their heads. As stated previously, the house we lived in was built by the agricultural department from the school system, as a project, similar to Habitat for Humanity. We did not have the best house, but it was not the worst either.

As stated in the chapter discussing business in the community, which will come later, we had many entrepreneurs, yet they did not survive beyond our generation due to limitations. Limitations that came from past issues or enforced from the "west side of the tracks."

Families in our neighborhood were never isolated. People seemed to care and actually show that they cared. As the history moves on, you will see how the lives changed and the caring ceased. The seeds planted later became a stumbling block to growth in our community. The seeds of greed, ingratitude, manipulation, and other things that grew in the community to cause people to stop caring for and giving to each other.

There were two-parent and there were single-parent families, most single-parent families were usually due to the death of a spouse. Very seldom did you hear or know of anyone that divorced. But as a child, we did not meddle in grown-folk business. We stayed in a child's place, doing childish things. The bottom line was that everyone in the community reached out to ensure that no one did without, as far as I could see. We may have lived in or had shacks, but as a community, what happened to one, happened to all. We pitched in to keep our community connected and safe. No one was left behind. We helped each other.

There was no city transportation for us across the tracks. The train came through the town, but it required money to ride and most used it to travel long distances. Some people had a horse and wagon used as transportation. My uncle owned a truck that transported workers to the fields to pull or chop cotton. The women who did domestic work outside the home were sometime transported by their employer. Others normally walked everywhere they needed to go.

The utilities of today were unheard of when I was growing up. There was electricity with the use of extension cords (not a lot of electrical outlets, and most people did not have electrical appliances). We used kerosene or coal oil lamps or lanterns for light. The majority of the houses did not have running water on the inside. For those that did not have indoor plumbing, there were wells in the yards. It was always a place to get a refreshing a drink that was always cool, and would quenched your thirst. When we visited the water fountain in town, there was one cup or canteen for all the blacks to use. During those times, you never worried about contamination issues, nor infections like you hear of today. We were not allowed to drink from the same fountain as the whites. Maybe they felt we were infected with something. But we never heard of people in the community having issues drinking from the same cup, water well, or fountain.

Again, we did not have indoor water, or plumbing. So all of our "bodily waste" business was done in the outhouse. We did not have the luxury of flushing a toilet as people have today. We had toilet cleaners that came to empty the waste every so often. People used sulfur to keep the foul smell down. Just reminiscing about this portion brings me to thinking about third world countries today. The illnesses they have because of sanitation issues. God's grace and mercy brought us through.

There was only one phone, on some streets in the neighborhood. My family had a phone and we did not mind sharing it. Sharing was a way of life in those days. There seemed to be more hospitality in those days. People had more patience. Sometimes a call would come through and you had to run to get the person from their house. The operator held on until you returned and while she held on, she could hear any and everything that went on. There was no way of having silence as you do today. And it was common for three or four other people to have the same line as you did. That was what was called a party line. Someone could pick up a phone at their house, while you were at your house talking. So if it was an emergency, out of courtesy, the phone was hung up. Everything is so computerized these days, I don't know if operators still exist. I know party lines do not exist because of privacy laws.

The fashion was unique. We had the opportunity to shop at some stores to buy clothes. There were some who probably obtained clothes from the people they worked for when it was no longer needed for their children. My wife, in her younger years before we were married, was a very skillful seamstress. This was a skill that she developed at an early age. She made men's suits, hats, and women's dresses. They were very elegant. She obtained material from the businesses in town. Some of the name brands have nothing on the talent that she did back then.

We had medical care in the community as well. My mom had a natural instinct for taking care of the sick and wounded. She was a midwife, which is different from a registered nurse. She had the expertise, knowledge and wisdom of a doctor. She worked under a doctor from the other side of the tracks. He helped and groomed her medical skills, what is called clinical expertise these days. He used her to take care of the blacks and the Hispanics in our community and other surrounding areas. She would take care of people and animals. There were many times I watched her use the red clay dirt to make a type of healing salve to place on wounds to draw out the soreness and infection.

Chapter 4:

##########

People in the Community

The people in the community were respectful. You had all types or shades of color, from dark-skinned to light-skinned, across the tracks, as in other areas of the town, state and nation. But as I stated earlier, you were either white (from the other side of the tracks) or you were black (from across the tracks and some other sections of the town).

The language was kind of a broken slang. Well, it wasn't slang to us. It was real talk. We understood each other. I guess it was what we heard from the previous generation. But when I was in high school and college, I learned the correct way to pronounce and enunciate words. Yet still today, some of the older generations use those words. The young folks don't always understand, and it's reciprocal. We don't always understand them. I recently asked some of the seminary class members if they knew what a "side-straddle-hop" was. More than half did because of their age. I had to explain to others that it was the same as a jumping jack. It's important that we improve as time moves on, yet do not forget where you came from, and how you arrived.

As stated in the introduction, we were not poor, we were "po!" So 'po' that we could not afford the last two letters, as I say with a smile. And along with "po" was "fo" for four; and "doo" for door. The "r" sound was left out of many words.

"Ain't" is the most inappropriate word, but we have used it so much, that it is now a part of the English dictionary. Ain't simply meant "I am not!" But if you spoke so proper, you were considered too sophisticated or from the other side of the tracks. Truth be told, many of the white folks used the same words or used them more than we did.

More examples: sho'nuff was the same as saying sure enough or showing agreement. And if you wanted to keep something a secret, you would hear someone say, "now this is twinks us." To translate – it was between you and me. And one never was concerned about missing out. By showing possession, it was not mine and yours, it was mine and "yurn." And you had the right to put things wherever you wanted, which people would say, "you just have stuff 'strode' all o'er the place." Or if it was taking up too much space, one might say, "and you just 'spwald' ever where." And if you were cold, you got some 'kiver' to cover yourself and stay warm.

When they came in from the field, many of them were "tard," which meant they were tired. We did not get spankings or whippings, we got "whooped." When you were about to start something or do something, you would hear someone say, "I'm fixin' nah or 'bout tah…" Or to sho'nuff say you're coming, you may hear this phrase: I "loul to" be there," which simply meant – "I will probably be there or show up." Or sometimes, it was done yesterday, or the common way to say back then was: "yesdiddy." A measure of time was gauged by the sun or when you ate. We had bre'fas, dinner, and supper. And to be more specific on time, some may say, "just a little before now" or "in a lil while." And if you really wanted someone to believe what you said without any doubt, just say "Iswanee," which was the same as saying "I swear to ya." A "heap" was a way a measuring a lot of something. Or a "dab" was just the opposite, a little of nothing. Out of respect for someone, you may hear someone saying "nome" which meant no ma'am or "naw sa" which meant no sir! Nare'(pronounce nair-ray) meant none. For example, "not nare' one of those chillun' had on shoes."

Sometimes, it was just in the enunciation of the letters in the word. And the letter "K" seemed to be easier to say. Some people don't read scripture, they read "Stripture." And when the scripture was "pert-near" or close to the truth, they would say, "lawd, a' mercy." Translation to – "Lord, have mercy!" And when in church, if the singing was awesome, one may say, "they sho' did sang!"

We have always had a way of putting emphasis on words and syllables. It may not make sense now, but it worked for us. They were not afraid or scared of anything, but they were "sked." "I will let you know da'rekly" translated to "I will tell you in a minute" or "you will hear it straight from me." The letters "shr" or "str" seemed to be difficult to pronounce. We did not have streets or street signs, but people would say "up the skreet," "I love the Lord with all my skrength," "He keeps me skrong." Other letters that seem to cause challenges was "th" and "er" especially when it came to saying mother, it usually came out "muddah," "sistah" or "brothah." "That" was pronounced "dat." When in conversation with the older generations, I can hear myself at times using the language from way back yonder (is also a biblical word). Yonder meaning long ago or a distance.

All the neighborhood parents raised each other's children. Everyone knew each other. When one family had, they shared with others in the community. People were very close to each other. When it was time to travel to pick cotton, entire families would travel together. We were usually jammed packed in a truck transported to the cotton fields for the season.

We had single family households, which consists of dad, mom and children. Some may have had extended families living in the homes, but I was not aware of how often that happened. There were generations of children continuing in the same patterns of life. There were no chances taken on living. Everyone was satisfied with life, and no one rocked the boat.

Our community was the epitome of love thy neighbor, no matter where they were or where they came from. I am not sure if anyone had time to keep up with the Jones' because we did not know what the Jones' looked like or what they had. So whatever the Jones' had, they were not willing to share with us anyway, nor were they helping us to get it, for sure they did not live in our neighborhood.

The children were respectful, because we were disciplined and our character was shaped when we were young. You were taught to address grown-ups by Mr., Mrs., or Miss with their last name, if you did not know them well, or their first name. You had to put a handle on their name. It was a sign of respect. Children were expected to stay in a child's place. In other words, you were not caught in grown people's conversation. You could not even sit in the room with grown folks, when they were talking. And if you looked like you were engaged or in a daze listening, sometimes you were awakened with a tap (slap) on your face. There were certain words we did not say as children, such as the word lie, fool, or funk. Those were like cuss words. I am not saying we did not try to break a few rules. It's in our nature to rebel, but we had sense enough not to push our luck around grown folks. As children, our job was to get an education and have fun. Some children had to work and help the family, but we were allowed to be children in our community. Whatever it took to keep the family together, each one did his/her part.

The women were respected and respectful. They dressed with dignity and class, even when they went to work. The older women took time to teach and train the young women to cook, clean, iron, do hair, teach, take care of children and do house chores. The women predominantly stayed home and kept the house. When they did work outside of the house, they worked to clean white folk's houses and care for their children. They did work in the cotton fields at times. Women held professional positions as teachers, secretaries, nurses or midwives, cooks and/or maids. Women dressed in modesty. Young girls wore the latest fashions, but nothing provocative or enticing to lure men. Older women wore the dresses or skirts below their knees and their blouses or shirts up around their necks. They did not wear sleeveless tops unless it was the appropriate dress or attire. In other words, no flesh was showing to advertise or invite anyone of the opposite sex, unless that was a way of life. There were some loose women in the community. And everybody knew who they were. The majority of the women in our community were classy with great reputations.

The men were strong physically and mentally. The men in my day worked to provide for their families. They did not always have degrees or certification for their trade, but they did what they had to do. They took charge of their families and did what was needed, whether black or white. Some women did work, but more of domestic capacity, which will be discussed later. Men worked outside the homes. You never heard of or knew a house-husband. That type of thing did not exist. Men did hard jobs. They did things that help them build muscle and character. They did not mind getting dirty. There was a rare occasion where the man was disable and could not work, but they had some type of income to take care of their household. Men knew how to clean up and look good. One other obvious thing in every community, you could tell the pastor from your average layman or male in the community. The pastor always wore a suit and stayed clean and presentable. I learned from many men in the community, especially my dad. The men of the city and community trained us. I never saw a man holding his wife's hand. We were taught to be hard and strong. You never saw a man embracing or kissing his wife. All of the public display of affection was done in secret. We were told as boys that men don't cry. You were taught to fight, not cry or show too much emotion. When you were caught crying, you were considered a wimp or punk back in those days. Crying was a disappointment to men. You never saw fathers hugging or consoling their sons or boys. Nor did you ever hear a man tell his son "I love you," at least not in front of anyone. As a matter of fact, I first embraced my daddy at the age of 30 something. When I did, I was drunk and wasn't sure if the meaning was clear and received very well.

The overall character of our community while I was growing up was a strong background of people that helped each other through hard times. We were not always taught specific scriptures, but in my wisdom glancing back, I see how our community rejoiced when others rejoiced and mourn when others mourned. It was a major task to take on the burdens of others. No one was left behind.

Across the Tracks

Jack WRat's Place

Chapter 5:

############

Business in the Community

I must say, that black people were entrepreneurs back in the day. We had the skills to run businesses and keep the community going. Almost every road had what we called a "beer joint." The beer joint was a place for socialization all during the day. But after sundown, it was for grown-ups only.

My parents owned a beer joint, called the Hilltop. It consisted of, what is called now-a-day, a bar and a café. My daddy knew how to make moonshine. I am sure there was a drinking age limit, as it is now. Due to religion and respect, you did not see many young people drinking like they do now. We respected our elders. We obeyed what they told us, whether it was our parents or not, we respected older people.

My parents did many other things just as others in the community. I realized that many of my business strategies and entrepreneurship came from my parents. I learned how to cook by watching my mom. My dad was a mattress maker, a shoe repair/maker, horticulture/gardener and he also worked for a millionaire in Rockdale. Sometimes, it is all about who you know, rather than what you know. My mother was a cook, a business woman, an advisor, and a midwife that delivered babies of all nationalities including whites, and Mexican nationals from the deep south in Texas. She was known throughout Texas.

There was competition in the community, yet it was not vicious competition that caused friction. Almost every street (according to the name) had a beer joint. On Third Street, was "The Last Chance" and "The White Front". On Bigger Street, was "Bell Place" and "Walton's Place", which was across the street from each other. On Fifth Street, "The Tin Top" and "Willis' Place", these were the places to be. All of these were black-owned businesses that catered to socialization and partying. There were also several beauty shops and barber shops.

My parents' place was open six days a week. Saturday night was a blast for everyone. All the cotton pickers would come in from the fields on weekends. My uncle owned a truck and would bring people to and from the cotton field. My job in the beer joint was to clean up all the beer bottles. I would sweep the floor and prepare for the next day of selling food and beer. I was not allowed in the place of business while grown-ups were drinking, nor during times of operation at night. No teenager was allowed in the establishment after dark. But we did sneak and peep into the windows a time or two, or as often as we could.

I learned a lot about life peeking through the windows of the family business. I watched my brother almost get killed. I observed things that helped me obtain street wisdom. And I even picked up a few bad habits of my own from observing. I watched fights with broken bottles and knives, as stated, never witnessed a murder, but came very close, as I watched through a window and saw my brother endure some serious injuries. These injuries were life threatening and left some severe challenges.

The area what we called the "Flats" was where the bulk of the people hung out. In the Flats was Pinky's grocery store and Jack Wrats store. It was similar to a convenient store. It had everything that we needed, but not as extensive as Pinky's.

Then there was Ledbetter's, a teenage place, which had fountain drinks. This was a place where we could dance, have ice cream, sodas, and other little snacks that were appeasing and palatable to teens. It was one form of entertainment for us.

On the corner of Third Street and Bigger was a mortuary. One thing is for sure, people will get sick and people will always die. So medical people and morticians are never without a job. As stated before, my mother was a midwife, so she took care of the sick in the community. Back in those days, sometime the "wake" would be held at the homes and the funeral would occur in the church about a week later after the death.

During my freshman year in high school, due to the advice of my uncle, the "Hilltop" became a teenage place to enjoy and have fun. I basically learned to become a business owner as a teenager. As stated earlier, my uncle picked up workers and transported them to south Texas to pick cotton (it was his business and one way of obtaining money). Every year during cotton season, which ran from May to about September and sometimes all the way to November, he would faithfully transport workers to the fields, of course for a fee. When the crop was over in south Texas, he would transport families to west Texas. He was also a banker and loan officer (put nicely). But to be honest, he was a loan-shark, who charged high interest. I mean very high interest. I learned to keep books and deal with money through him. I never had to pick cotton. I did it to keep up with others in the community. I made it my business to learn to cook and stitch mattresses.

After awhile, people seemed to make more money. The life of our community changed when businesses started to move in to town. There was no longer a need for laborers to pick cotton. There was a shift in our way of living. People became more independent. They no longer depended on each other. The mentality of giving decreased dramatically. It went from no-one-doing-without way of life to my-four-and-no-more or my-two-and-I'm-through type mentality.

The competitive spirit rose up and affected everyone in the community. When did the caring stop? Where did this mean spirit come from? Why such a drastic change? I did not have the answers at the time. In my spiritual knowledge, now I know it was spirits of jealousy and error. But whatever or however it happened, it was designed to keep us in the dump and to keep us separated within our own neighborhood. It was a plan to keep us in the dark, and it crippled many to stay in darkness. No one was willing to bring in light and better the community. I don't think they really knew how. Some that may have known how seemed to be limited in what they could do.

I knew there were frustrating times. The unsuccessful efforts led to frustration. Many did not understand that the frustration was designed to take their mind off the vision. When they took their mind off the vision, it pushed them to a point of further lack and desperation. They only could see for the moment. The frustration hindered the growth of the community. The businesses started to dwindle and families began to move out of Rockdale. More money was being made, but no one was sowing back into the community.

The faith was gone. Just as the word says, "without faith, it is impossible to please God" and "faith without works is dead."

Across the Tracks

Chapter 6:

##########

Church Life in the Community

Church life for me was excellent. Notice, I stated church life, not Christianity. There is a difference. Church life was excellent, because I never saw anything that would cause disgrace to the community. Communities and youth make a difference when you are brought up with discipline and church life. There were three main churches in the community – Allen African Methodist Church, New Hope Missionary Baptist Church and Springfield Missionary Baptist Church. New Hope Missionary MBC was the largest black church in the town, when I was growing up. There was a holiness church that was run by a woman. Back in our day and still in some churches, women were not allowed in the pulpit, let alone pastor a church. That was not part of God's plan or so we thought or how we were taught in some churches. My wife's uncle pastored a church here and would come to town and have a revival at different times. People would attend and some would stand outside and peep in the windows just to watch people in the congregation dance and "be filled with the Holy Ghost."

We did not have church service every Sunday. New Hope MBC had service every 2nd and 4th Sunday, and Springfield had service every 1st and 3rd Sunday of the month. I guess we did not have church every Sunday, because we did not have a pastor that lived in the community. They usually pastored several churches to make a decent living. But we did have Sunday School every Sunday.

The organizational structure of the church was from highest ranking to layman – Pastor, deacons, secretary & treasurer, Sunday School teachers, missionaries, ushers and other laymen. Since the pastor was not there every Sunday or for Sunday School, the other officers took charge to ensure the church business was run properly, according to what they knew. The pastor was elected by the members, not based on knowledge on the Word of God, or lifestyle, but based on how loud and long he could holler. It worked for the community back then, but as I have become wiser, I cannot understand how one could pastor and not live in the same community as your members. Nor how was it possible to pastor several churches at one time. That was like having two wives or taking care of two houses. That was a seed that was planted, which still affects our churches today. Pastors hold full-time jobs and are expected to care for the church members and their families.

The order of protocol on Sundays was in this fashion: Sunday school was approximately 9:00 AM or 10:00 AM. Church service would follow at 11:00 AM and could last to about 2:00 PM. When service is every other Sunday, the pastor had a lot to say and rebuke, I say it jokingly. But in hindsight, it may have been truth hidden in there somewhere. In the evening, there was Baptist Training

Union or famous BTU. The teachers for Sunday School and BTU were usually the same teachers in school. They were usually older women, which was good, because they had experience and wisdom to teach others. They taught young men to teach the younger boys and make them responsible as mentors. They taught young girls to teach and keep records to groom them. It showed consistency within the schools, churches and community. When you knew and saw the same people, you already knew what to do and how far to go. There was no such thing as disrespecting a teacher.

When we did have church service, the order of service has not changed much today as it was then. We had devotion, which consisted of a hymn and a prayer. When devotion began, you would hear someone belt out – Guide me oh thy Great Jehovah, Pilgrim through this barren land! And the congregation would repeat in unison: guide-----me----oh, Thy--------gre----a----t-----Je-----ho---vah--------Pil-----grim----through this----------ba------ren--------laaaaannnnnndd. And if they really wanted to show how much they knew, they would continue with – I am weak, but Thy art mighty. Hold me with Thou powerful hand! And the congregation would blend in – I--------am-----weak, but---------Thy------art-----mi----ghty-----hold-----me-----with, thou----------pow-----r'ful------haaannnd. And if the Holy Ghost really hit, you may hear it louder with – Bread of heaven! Bread of heaven! Feed me till I want no more! Bread------ of------hea'vn-------Bread---------of--------hea------ven--------feeeeed-------me-----unnn-------til, I-------want--------no----more! ---------

After the hymn, some deacon would pray. It must have been a requirement for deacons to know a hymn and pray. Every deacon had the line in his prayer, "Lord, give us that love that runs from heart to heart and from breast to breast." And "thank You that my bed was not my cooling board." You never heard them pray the word of God back to Him. But the majority of the deacons somehow were not found in devotion. They were found under the tree smoking. Yet they seemed to make it in the church just before the preacher preached. But you had some faithful deacons. Sometimes they would break out with the hymn, "Must Jesus bear the cross alone and all the world go free? No, there's a cross for everyone and there's a cross for me."

There were a few issues with our leaders back in the day, but for the most part, they were respectful and well respected. They carried themselves decently in the community. They took care of the church because of the infrequency of the pastor.

When devotion was over, the choir was in charge. It was nothing like today. The choir wore robes. There was unity and dignity. We only had a piano, when I was growing up. Later, we did get an organ, and it was much later. I will leave that alone for now. Some types of behavior within the church can be out of order, and the wisdom God has imparted upon me, He does things decent and in order. Back to the choir, they sang songs that were meaningful. There was not a lot of music to cover up the voices. We had gifted, talented singers that seem to sing from their heart. There were times of some infiltrating for selfish gain. It's human to want to take God's glory for self.

After the choir prepared the congregation, the pastor was ready to preach the word. The pastor was elected by the members, and he did not leave until he died or was fired. As stated earlier, it was based on how long and loud he could whoop and holler. Service was longer because we only met every other Sunday and he had to get us right enough to last for two weeks. I do not remember any sermons. Nor do I remember scripture being taught. I just remember a lot of screaming, deep breathing and sweating. One thing I must say, the preacher did preach the hell out of us. They preached fire and brimstone back then. Yet no one ever taught us how to avoid the fire and brimstone of hell.

Once the sermon was complete, there was a period for joining the church. That was when you gave the preacher your hand and supposedly the Lord your heart. During this period, I do not remember the preacher ever discussing repentance nor praying for salvation to enter a person's heart. We called it joining church, because that was all it was. It was the time when a person could have their name placed on the church roll. It had no merit to whether they were saved or accepted Christ as their Savior. I never heard it mentioned about coming to Christ, nor praying the repentance prayer. To know what I know now, I am sad that many were not really converted or saved to really know Christ as their personal Savior. If it was the case, there should have been a thirst for the word of God. There would have been a hunger for righteousness. There would have been change in the community. People can only do what they know. Had the pastor known better and truly understood the needs of the people, maybe more lives would have been changed.

After the period of joining the church, the offering was taken up by the deacons. It was not received, but taken. We were never taught about tithing and offering. We paid according to Tribes, which consisted of $2 a Sunday. After the offering was taken up, the amount was announced. This was specific for the pastor's salary. I am not sure how other bills were paid or other things in the church were taken care of. Somehow God made a way. As I think back to the word of God, the community was cursed with a curse. Few may have brought their tithes, which is only a 10th of your first fruit. As I reminisce, I can see how the community put everything and everyone before God, to include their money. We did not trust God with what belonged to Him. We were not obedient. But how can you be obedient to what you do not know? The seeds planted are still being reaped by poverty.

We had the benediction and closed out in song – "Bless be the ties that bind our hearts in Christian love. The fellowship of kindred minds is like to that above." We never really fellowshipped after church. The pastor was taken care of by the women of the church. He would rotate to a different house every Sunday. One thing for sure, Sunday was respected by the community. The beer joints were not open.

Everything was closed on Sunday. Even the winos covered their bottles when passing the church yard or cemetery. There was a type of respect for the church, no matter what religion. It was out of reverence for God.

We have lost so many values within the church community. The pastor use to hold the title of Reverend. They should have been called Pastors more than reverend as an initiation to the position or the office. Whatever you call him, that is what he will be. Calling them what they were would have instilled in them their true calling and not just a title, back then. This was according to Ephesians 4:11. Pastor is a gift to the church, which is out of initiation. Reverend is out of respect, not a gift. Now, they are called pastor or minister, which is ok, but the scripture was taken out of context to cause people to change their way of recognizing the man of God. The Bible talks about reverencing God and not man, but it was referring or intent for meaning out of action, not a title according to the word. People have taken the word of God and twisted it to provide them a way of escaping responsibility and obedience.

As stated above, there is so much value that has been lost in the church today, compared to when I grew up. People respected the way they dressed to respect the Lord's house. You never saw men or women wearing shorts in church, (Flip flops were not invented then) and everyone wore appropriate shoes. Too much flesh and skin showing has caused distraction from the body of Christ to the physique of man and woman. Men did not wear hats in the church. "Come as you are" did not mean to lose respect for God's house. People have taken a heart condition and turned it into physical means that sometimes disgraces the church. In addition to dressing, movement in the church has become excessive and distracting. Children did not go to the restroom as often as they do now. Children did not have children's church. Children were taught to be still and be quiet. We did not see leaders or believers bringing Bibles to church. So all we had to go on, was what the pastor was preaching or what he told us.

Now, there were other services that went on within the church. Every year there was Pastor's Anniversary, Choir Anniversary, Usher Day, Missionary Day, Children's Day, and your normal holidays where we had an influx of people coming for Easter and Mother's Day. We also had what was called Rally Day, where we would have fund raisers by selling cakes, pies, plate lunches, and whatever else was decided. This was money used to improve the church. And there were also annual revivals that started on Sunday night and lasted the entire week, until Friday. We also had Association Meetings, which was all the churches coming together and having services.

I am not saying in this portion that our church was 100% right, nor am I condemning their choices, but I know they tried. They lived the life they knew as best they could with what they had. It seemed like the members did not tried to seek more knowledge or a clearer understanding, because the pastor and leaders were revered as knowing what was best. No one challenged nor tried to change what was taught or emulated.

Across the Tracks

Chapter 7:

############

Social Life in the Community

One thing was for sure, we may not have had much, but we knew how to be grateful for what we had and how to enjoy life. We had a movie theater in the town called the Dixie Theater. We were allowed to go to what we called the picture show to see a movie on the big screen. The blacks had to sit in the balcony. The cost for the movie was nine cents. There was no restroom available for the blacks to use on the inside. If you left during the movie to go to the restroom, you had to pay to get back in, however we would sneak back in. One would hold the door to allow the other in and run up the long steps to the balcony. Once we got in, how would they know who had paid or not. There was no such thing as getting popcorn or snacks for our folks. The blacks were not allowed to have service from the snack area. As time progressed, in the 1950's, a more modern theater was opened, but it was still segregated. We were again limited on what we could do.

There was not a lot for teens to do in the community. One thing for sure, as teenagers, being put in jail was out of the question. The thing we would do to get in trouble was trivial. We would play in some of the teachers and farmers yards. For entertainment, we would throw rocks on top of tin roof houses and run and raid gardens and fruit orchards. There wasn't anything or much to steal on the east side. I cannot recall teens getting drunk or on any substance abuse drugs. Parents would not stand for any of that foolishness. It was considered disrespect or a disgrace to the family name. And that was not an option.

I learned quite a bit from my uncle on my mom's side. Most of the things I learned (as stated previously) was from sneaking and peeking through the windows of the beer joints. To me, that was entertainment. I learned how to dance (or what they called gyrating, back then) and listened to great music. I saw fights, I mean some major knock-down, drag-outs. I never saw anyone get shot, but I saw many knife fights in my day. I learned much vulgarity. My dad was an expert at cussing. I did not want to be like that, but I found myself gravitating to that type of lifestyle without much effort.

My dad was also abusive. He was a violent man. Most men were in those days. It was passed down through the generations, and women seemed to tolerate it. I watched as it affected my brother and his family. I found that anger is a learned attitude. There are some things you have to learn to control and eliminate from your life. As I grew more knowledgeable in the Word of God, I realize the ungodly spirits that plagued our family, our community, our way of life.

We did not have a television until I was about 16 years old. There was no form of entertainment like children have today. My parents were among the first black singers to perform on radio in the city. They were very good singers, but that was one talent that I did not receive. I did play a trumpet in the band at school. I was about 9 years old, when the school formed a band, and it was an exciting time. We performed and brought excitement to the community. We were more entertaining than the football game. Around the time that I was 15 or 16, our band director had us playing in beer joints. I quit participating in the band when I started to excel in football. We did have neighbors that had television. The major thing was boxing in those days, so we would visit with the neighbors to watch boxing matches.

During certain times of the season, the boys in the neighborhood would hunt and swim. We swam in tanks or small ponds. So whenever and however we needed to have fun, we would find a way. We were normal children, growing up in the neighborhood living a life of pleasure with no cares in the world. We knew how to have a good time.

There were many celebrations throughout the year. The 19th of June celebration was always big. According to history, Juneteenth marked the end of the war and enslaved people were free. This news was out of Galveston, Texas, two and a half years after President Lincoln signed the Emancipation Proclamation.

New clothing was brought for children to wear for that day. Children would have a good time just playing at the fair park. Grown-ups would get into fights, throwing beer bottles during the dance. People came from all around the country to celebrate. My parents would always sell hamburgers with the stands set up, like a concession stand. It was the official end of slavery in the United States. We celebrated, but I wonder how many were really free? Not free physically, but as I have reminisced and reviewed the history of Rockdale, many were still enslaved in their mindset, their way of living, and their day-to-day routines.

Then there were cotton picking time. This was when it was time to plant, pick, chop, or harvest cotton crops. It was a time to work, yet it was an enjoyable time as those who had to travel, picked up the entire family and went off to work. See in the next chapter, more details of work life in Rockdale. The cliché: "all work and no play make Jack a dull boy" was not important during our culture. We worked, and we played. As long as the job was done, we enjoyed ourselves. It was a way of life.

Across the Tracks

Chapter 8:

##########

Work Life in the Community

There were job opportunities in the town, but blacks did not have the same opportunity to prosper as whites did. When some blacks did have the opportunity to work, they were limited to what they could do and how far they advanced. One thing you never saw was a black in charge of a white, no matter what the age. It wasn't unusual seeing a young white boy in charge of a more mature black man. That was the norm back then, even if one had advanced education. He or she was smart enough or enticed to stay where they could advance and possibly rise to management positions.

Work life across the tracks consisted of cotton picking and chopping, hay hauling, watermelon loading, chicken picking, janitorial work, dishwashing, cooking and later with a Large Company moving in, plant work, truck driving, heavy equipment operating and whatever businesses that were owned in our community. Some were blessed to go to places of higher learning and obtain advanced education, in order not to become a laborer. I was one of those, and God has blessed me to give back to the community.

There were odd jobs in the community such as farming, but that was solely owned by the white man. I knew of one black farmer in our community. But there was not much prosperity at that time. There were blacksmiths and carpenters that lived on both sides of the tracks, and I know of only one black plumber.

There was a millionaire in the town. He had a contract making broughams or Army boots for the military. That's how my dad learned his trade to repair and sole shoes. My dad worked for this millionaire and learned every trade or skill that he could to teach and train us and others, or just basically to take care of our family. Whatever the reason, he did what he had to do, and he did a great job. The millionaire also had contracts with University of Texas and Texas A&M to do concession sells. My dad learned how to do concession work. I am sure that helped him to run the beer joint he owned in the community.

Now the main job that was meant for us as blacks was cotton picking. When cotton picking time came around, (as stated before, yet now in more detail) my uncle would transport people, who were called load-up hands. The load-up hands would get into a ½ ton truck, sometimes whole families – men, women, and children approximately 40 – 50 people per transfer, and travel to lower south Texas to pick cotton. Once in the field, there was about 70 – 100 people on site to work. It was about a 12 – 15-hour drive from Rockdale to the location. The work of chopping cotton was different than picking it. When chopping, children made the same wages as grown-ups, by the hour. As told by one of the members of the current church, the pay was about 30 cents a day. But when picking cotton, everyone was paid by the weight of what they picked, so it was more paid by the pound. Children were given croaker-sacks to pick and carry their loads easier. There were two different camps in south Texas, but they belonged to the same white man.

Upon arrival to the destination, there were shacks set up as sleeping quarters. Picking cotton was not just a day trip. Sometimes, families stayed for weeks at a time. We did not have beds to sleep on. Everyone slept on the floor. There were no air conditioners. Windows were prop open with sticks to let air circulate. We got up early to start the day's tasks. By lunch time, we were prepared to eat. We would eat under the truck in the shade. Our lunch consists of sardines and bologna with crackers. The worse part of lunch was keeping the flies away from your sardines. We had tin cups for drinking water. The women stopped earlier in the evening to start preparing dinner. The men continued to work until sundown.

It amazed me that there were many amenities even when we went to pick cotton. It was as though they catered to what they thought we wanted. In the nearest town, there was a movie theater or a place to see a picture show. There was a beer joint where people could drink. There was what we called a Victrola or a juke box that played records and the people danced to the music. I remember asking my mom, "they have everything else to entertain us, but where is the church?" She did not have an answer. Another seed planted in the lives of our people to put work and entertainment before God. His word is still the same yesterday, today and forever more. At that time, I was not aware of Matthew 6:33, "Seek ye first the Kingdom of God and His righteousness, and all these things shall be added unto thee." As I am older, I realize that no one in our community was aware of that scripture. Even today, people feel the need to put money and work ahead of or in the place of God. The hustle-and-grind mentality will not change until there is a realization that God will not come second to anything.

Across the Tracks

Chapter 9:

##########

School Life in the Community

I must say that we had the best teachers in our school system. I attended elementary or grade school on the same site where the current Institute for Teaching God's Word is located. We called it Pre-primer back in the day. That was like a head start or kindergarten for us. My first few years of school, everyone was in one classroom, no matter the age. As we grew in years, we started to have separate classes and grades.

The teachers truly loved their jobs. They not only taught us, they also took care of us. The teachers in school were usually the same teachers in Sunday School. They were very disciplined in their character and reputation. You never saw a teacher looking like a student. The women were dressed with dignity and class. You never heard of teachers courting or having sexual relations with students. They had ethical values in our schools.

There was one professor (or principal) in our school that was sometimes called an "Uncle Tom." Back in my day that was a derogatory name for a black man that catered to the white man. He seemed to do whatever he was told and would not stick up for himself or others. People said an uncle

Tom had no backbone to defend himself, even when he was right. Many would say he was "eating cheese." That was described as smiling in the face of a white person and afraid to speak up for the rights of others or yourself. But there were times when the gentleman was not being an Uncle Tom or eating cheese, he was sacrificing his dignity for the students. If he bucked the system or stood up to them, he would have been released, harmed or maybe killed. Then we as student would have gotten someone who may not have cared as much for us. He did what was needed to help us learn more and survive. Some of us even thrived. He really pushed us to the limits, and quite often beyond our limitations. I can never recall having a bad day at school. My wife may have a different perspective. She was three years behind me.

We seldom had discipline issues. You were disciplined by anyone in the community. If you were caught doing wrong, you were disciplined right there on the spot. And when you got home, you were disciplined again for being disciplined. I wonder how the news beat us home. We did not have cell phones back then. The only way of communication was word of mouth and the one telephone that everybody used.

I remember cheating on an exam before. I really did not have to, but for some reason I did. My mom came to the school and confronted the teacher. I was in 7th grade at the time. I made a "C" and my mom was convinced that I didn't cheat. The teacher begged to differ. My mom insisted that I retake the test at that moment. I was scared, but I had a good memory. When the test was over, I aced it! I guess my mom believed that I was not just average. Cheating on that test caused me to get a lower grade. If my mom had not challenged that teacher, what turn would my life have taken? It is important for parents to be a part of their children's education. Take time to meet the teachers and monitor the homework and tests.

As I attended high school. I became more involved in sports. It was my junior and senior year that I began to thrive. In1959, I was voted the Best Athlete, Most Talented, and School Spirited, which was listed in Aycock High Yearbook. I participated in football, basketball, track and summer baseball, and served as captain for all sports during my senior year.

In football, as a Junior – 1959, I held positions as receiver, defensive back, punter, placekicker, punt returner and kickoff return. During that season, the team only lost one game. We had the second best record in Aycock School history. The team could have won the district championship, but was disqualified. In 1960, as a Senior and captain of the team, held positions of running back, quarterback, punter, placekicker, defensive back, and kickoff return. That year, I rushed for over 200 yards in five different games. The leading scorer in the district. As a quarterback, I was told by my Coach to run the ball every play until the opposing team stops you, because I was not an accurate passer.
In basketball, the years of 1959 & 1960, I was often the point guard, with a good jump and set shot. I started out in 1959 as fast-break point guard on second string. As a senior, I

was a starter on the team averaging 16 points per game with the ability to dunk at the stature height 5 feet 10 inches. I was usually guarded by the tallest opposing player because of my vertical leap.

In track, the year of 1959, I was a part of the relay champion team. The team (with their time listed) consisted of Arthur Locklin (9.8), James Maloy (9.9), Freddie Smith, (10.6), Dennis Brooks (9.8), all running great times in their heat. Although we were disqualified in the relay, we remained undefeated. I also participated in the long jump, high jump, 200 & 110 hurdles. In 1960, I participated in the 200 & 110 hurdles, missing out on becoming district champion by falling at the last hurdle. I also participated in the sprint relay, high jump, and long jump.

In summer baseball, I wasn't very good as a pitcher, but excelled in every other position, from the season of 1959 – 1960. The teammates knew me as a person who stayed in extreme physical condition, and would always report in excellent condition – thanks to Billy Ray Locklin.

I was Salutatorian of the 1960 graduating class and received the Dare Award. I did not want to leave school. I loved it so much growing up that I cried because I graduated. It truly had an impact on my life. I will always remember the quote from Professor Wilhite, "Son, allow your legs to pay for your education." However, I did not listen because my passion was not in football. I also thank Mrs. Susie Piper for encouraging and standing by me, as well as insisting that I do the right thing. She continues to push me, even now. I received scholarship offers from – Prairie View

A&M, Bishop College, Paul Queen, Saint Phillips, New Mexico State.

My heart was to join the Army, following the path of my brothers. After failing the physical in four different branches, I accepted the scholarship to New Mexico State. By that time, my passion for football was gone. From a spiritual standpoint, I wasn't sure if football was my gift or talent, or something that others groomed me for or to push me in a direction that they preferred. I have come to understand true spiritual gifts and natural talents. Some people are gifted with certain talents, but it is not necessarily a gift to the body of Christ. The scripture states in Psalms 18:16, "your gifts will make room for you and bring you before great men." The gift incorporated with passion and the will to do it can and will bring overall benefits. One without the other can lead to failure and regret.

I later enrolled at the American school of marketing in San Francisco, and graduated in 1962. I also attended El Centro College for two years, majoring in business administration. I was a participant in the kicking Caravans, put on the by the Dallas Cowboys in 1967, they were recruitment kickers for professional football, but I walked away. I had a greater call upon my life, and I had a yearning for something different. I could not join the military, no matter how hard I tried or how many attempts. God had something else in store for me. During this time in my life, I wasn't sure what it was, I knew I wanted to make money and take care of my family. In the years to come, it was clear what God's plan was for my life. Jeremiah 29:11 was definitely God speaking directly to me.

Chapter 10:

##########

The Change – 1952 The Large Company Shift

In the 1950's, there was a shift in our community. Several large plants moved into Rockdale. It was the beginning of change, an opportunity to make money, which was a good thing. But it was also the change that drove the values of some out of the community. During those times there were minority owned businesses across the tracks. When these companies moved in, the business of working started to own us. There was a subtle mental shift. The job of working became more than a way of life, it began to control lives in a negative way. Instead of taking charge of the job, the job took charge of the lives and the community. Gradually, the change switched the focus of getting out of poverty physically, but continuing with the same mindset. A few years after integration started, most were just excited to go over the tracks, where we had restrictions before. Instead of focusing on getting out, we should have kept our focus on moving up and not out. The money could still be made and build up businesses within our communities instead of taking it completely out and starving the community. The hiring practices for minorities were already bad enough. When they were hired, it was a select few and there were limitations on what position you could work. Most of the positions were janitors or lower end of pay positions.

ACROSS tHE TRacKs

To some these companies were known as a curse to our town and to our community. You were limited to advancing. The objective seemed to come across as improving the way of living, but not enough to help you make it out of your current situation. Attitudes were changing. Mentality was drifting more towards alcoholism and further poverty. After integration, there were still beer joints that seem to thrive – during the early 50's, but now they were on the other side of the track, because of the money and people from other counties coming in to buy. During segregation times, men began to dessert their families, which was the beginning of an increased stronghold. Money, which should have gone home, went for good times.

From 1952 to 1954, big money was made by blacks, but little was put back across the tracks. There was a bad seed planted in the minds of people across the tracks. Where we live was a place to leave behind and not fix up. No more sowing money into your own community. They did not feel like it was worth much. But, I disagree. They did not see the value. All land is good. Earth has already been established, and God is not creating any more land. It is our duty, according to God's word in Isaiah 61:4, which says they shall build the OLD WASTE; they should raise up the former desolation, and they shall repair the waste cities, the desolation of many generations (my emphasis on "old waste").

I challenge everyone that reads this book to take Isaiah 61:4 literally, to go back to your roots and do something to change your community. Remember the waste. Focus on the waste. Some have come back, but did not change the community. Do not just take it to the other side of the track just to make money or upkeep what is already in place or fixed. Fix up where you came from. You cannot and should not leave your roots behind.

For some strange reason, people did not sow back into the community. When the workers were off, they had places to drink and party outside of the neighborhood. So in turn, businesses were lost. The upkeep of the community was worse. No one cared to help like they did before.

If one were to excel in industry, they were soon released or demoted to keep them from advancing too quickly for fear of moving to the top and becoming decision makers. There were several that did make it out of the community to become successful in life. They owned property, had farms, continued to have successful businesses, some even worked on the city council. But once successful, they moved to "the other side of the tracks," in some instances, physically and many times, only in their minds. I can only imagine what their thoughts were, but based on action, they believed it would change them and their way of life. Yet, very few came back to improve or help those left across the tracks, which could have led to more improved living quarters or a better way of life for future generations. As stated earlier in the book, sometimes, captivity of the mind can be worse than physical bondage.

Chapter 11:
##########

Now – The Transition and Transformation

Here I am, right where God wants me to be. As I look back over my life, and I think things over. I can truly say that I have been blessed. I have a testimony. We overcome by the blood of the Lamb and the word of our testimony. I can see the plan God had for my life, as well as when the transition took place.

I was not really active in church. I attended when I could, and did not hold positions nor work actively on a committee. But one day, God pricked me to change. I was financially successful in the world. I had a new house, new cars, and plenty of land with everything a man could ever want or dream. I had about 50 acres of land with 30-40 head of cattle, 25-30 hogs, and other assets for investments. I seem to have it all, but I was not in right relationship with God. Oh, I had been baptized and gave my hand to the preacher, but I was not born again. I knew nothing about salvation or its requirements, at the time. I was lost until I was 36 years old.

One night in a dream, the Lord showed me who I really was. I saw the Lord high on a mountain, beckoning people to come. As He beckoned, I came. It was a multitude of people and as they approached Him, they were separated like lamb and goats. As I came closer, He looked at me and said, "depart from Me, I know you not." I was confused. I joined the church at an early age. I was a faithful church member. I attended church regularly. I was transformed in that process, because I realized that I wasn't going to heaven.

I isolated myself in Waco, TX for 10 months. Oh, I continued to work as normal, but I did not do the things I use to do. I began to read the Word of God. I had read the Bible completely at age 19, but I did not understand the scripture. At this point, I read 10 chapters a day, and I begin to pray. No one ever taught me how to pray the word of God back to Him. So He took my baby speech, understood my heart and delivered me. I realized that God will talk to you and teach you through His word, if only you are willing to listen. A passage of scripture comes to mind now that helps me to see the work God did during that time of isolation. First John 2:27 says, "But the anointing which ye have received of Him abideth in you, and ye need not that any man teach you: but as the same anointing teacheth you of all things, and is truth, and is no lie, and even as it hath taught you, ye shall abide in Him." As I read and learned the Word of God for myself, the anointing was being poured over me. There was a change. I was truly born-again. I knew a minister working within the company that stayed a few doors down from me in the same hotel. I went to him with my story, and he led me to the Christ, the right way. It is amazing what God can and will do. We made fun of this minister about the God he served. And at that time, God sent me to him so he could lead me through the steps of salvation. This was similar to Paul on Strait Street with Ananias.

I later returned to New Hope and told the people what happened. They told me to get ready that I would be preaching my first sermon soon. What? That is not what I expected. I did not like it. I did not want to preach. I did not have the same expectations of preaching the way the pastors did it. But I did what they told me to do, out of respect. I preached my first sermon, and I did not hoop or holler. You know that hooping and hollering was how preachers seem to get their point across to the people. I was instructed by God to use a different method. I taught the word. I spoke directly from the Word of God, just as He instructed.

My calling was accepted by the people, but not without ridicule or criticism. I did not know all that was said, but I heard many whispers and repeats of what others said. Once the word of my accepting the calling got out in the community, people stated they wanted to come to see if it was true. They wanted to know what happened to Dennis. It's amazing when you change and people still want to remember you for how you use to be. What I use to do, they know I did it with class. Now it wasn't that I changed, but my change was going to affect them. Now some things that I use to do, I could not and would not do anymore.

It was amazing that Springfield MBC saw the difference in me and not just heard a difference. It was 1978, when I was called by God to minister. A year later, I was pastor at Springfield. I was a novice minister. I didn't know anything about pastoring. We were still meeting every other Sunday. And I expressed to them that God did not just want them to assemble every other Sunday. He wanted them in church every Sunday. The word stated to forsake **not** the assembly.

I told them that I would be in church preaching every Sunday whether they were there or not. Within a few months, they started attending every Sunday. They accepted me for who I was, and the change that was needed. I did not go in complaining or attempting to condemn them for what they had been doing for decades or all of their lives. I just went in with a transformed and renewed mind after God changed my heart. God showed me the needs, and I went about my Father's business to meet the needs individually and collectively.

I was there for about 5 years. My initial task was to teach adults the books of the Bible. This is the primary responsibility of knowing the word of God. Every born again believer should know how to find scripture and know the books of the Bible. Yet again, I did not complain, belittle, nor scold. I just did what God sent me to do, and that was to teach. Teach is what I did. Teaching does not require hooping and hollering.

I taught series such as tithes and offerings, major issues and characters in the Bible, as well as the books of the Bible. We all grew in the knowledge of the Lord. We learned and moved higher, while the Lord continued to bless and take us higher.

God is still in the blessing business. After leaving, Springfield, God instructed me to move away from tradition of religion and step into building relationships. My wife and I started with Bible Study in our home. It grew rapidly from 8 to 36 people within a few months. We knew we needed to find a building, because our home could not hold very many people in one room.

God gave me the vision to build a school to teach His people. Breaking ground for Institute for Teaching God's Word in 1985 and completed in 1986. We did not have enough money to build. I donated the land that was purchased for a night club, which was to consume a complete city block. The collateral we had was worth more than $800,000, but we were refused a $100,000 loan. I knew enough at that time that God would provide. He would not have given me the vision, if He was not going to give me the provision. And provide, He did. We were granted a loan from outside of the city. The city where I grew up, returned with my family to live, paid taxes and frequented businesses, did not have trust or faith in my business skills to help me move forward.

We started with the small building located on Mulberry Street, which is now the American Academy of Crisis Counseling (AAOCC) Releasing the Sound School of Fine Arts. This site is predominately geared towards after school and summer programs. It is designed to meet the needs of the community youth, ages eight to 17, in education musical enrichment, life skills and awareness programs that do not place limitation on bicultural values, norms and traditions, but interrupts the onset and prevalence of drug use, abuse and illiteracy.

The program provides students with tools that are necessary for sustaining and abundant life through counseling, vocational and life skills training in an inclusive environment; to provide a holistic approach in addressing the needs of those typically under-served; and to counsel with those who have experience coping with difficulties.

The purpose of AAOCC is to provide Faith-based crisis counseling to religious, charitable Christian education, philanthropic and benevolent purposes; and provide a biblically-based counseling resource to train caregivers in crisis intervention. Oftentimes, underserved and at-risk-youth believe that abuse (sexual assault, domestic violence, dating violence and stalking) is simply not happening in their rural communities because they never talk about it. In reality, if youth, parents and community are not talking about their experiences, it is usually because parents, the community and faith leaders have not created an atmosphere in which it is safe to disclose.

Not long after the establishment of the School, we established the church – "New Jerusalem Interdenominational Church. The main thrust of this movement is to train men and women in the Word of God and send them forth to reach the lost with the good news that Jesus saves. The curriculum of the School Institute for Teaching God's Word (ITGW) focuses on practical applications that are needed to meet the needs of the growing church of today. Students will not lose experience gained through church attendance, program participation, auxiliary functions and evangelism. All of these tasks help to enhance the growth of the church.

This particular seminary operated on the belief that biblical training can be achieved outside the traditional classroom. The entire program is designed so that students will have the freedom to study within the pastoral context and setting. The local church becomes a "learning laboratory" in which skills can be demonstrated and tested under the guidance of experienced pastors and church leaders.

The seminary has seen more than 15,000 students over the course of years in existence. There have been numerous graduating classes that include some top named artists and ministers throughout the United States, as well as Africa and Europe. We have truly been blessed to continue the work that God gave to me as a vision so many years ago.

Now, we have advanced to provide a business in the community. Sho'Nuff Soul Food Diner is a restaurant established in 2012 on the grounds that was originally a night club. Sho'Nuff is more than a soul food diner and non-profit organization; it's a piece of history and a combination of culture and heritage, family and community, food and life! Since its inception, Sho'Nuff has existed to bless the lives of individuals while rebuilding, feeding, and helping the community. We believe in change and second chances. The employment opportunities with Sho'Nuff are opened to everyone. Our mission is to employ men and women who may have a criminal history that may be a hindrance in finding gainful employment in their pursuit to becoming a positive, productive member of their family and our community.

Sho'Nuff Soul Food management takes rebuilding the community literally. We commit to demolishing or remodeling old buildings in the surrounding community. We construct new buildings to host new programs and incubate businesses that will be a blessing to the community. We believe that a person can learn beyond circumstance. We are committed to training persons who have an interest in pursuing a career in restaurant service and management through the Soul Food Culinary Training Program.

So it takes vision and a plan to work the vision according to God's word in order to succeed. According to Isaiah 61:4, I have made it my mission to improve the waste city where I grew up. It has been desolation. There is still work to be done, but I pray that others who came from this town will give back and improve our community to help it thrive.

Across the Tracks

The Challenge
##########

"Across the Track" Challenge:

I would like to **challenge** everyone who grew up in Rockdale, TX across the tracks to sow seeds within the community to advance our community. Those who benefited from those who lived across the tracks, by their toil and labor, maybe you who read this book might say, "I didn't grow up across the tracks, however my grandparents did hire workers from across the tracks." Hopefully, you will fill in on their behalf, and sow into the community as well. I am not asking anyone to move back, unless the Holy Spirit leads you to return. If that is prompting you to move back, just know that God will provide.

Within this **challenge**, I ask that you provide financial means to help Rockdale "across the tracks" to grow. The financial means could be in providing a business "across the tracks," in which the funds will remain in the town. Or invest in other businesses that will help advance the wealth and upkeep of what is needed to thrive "across the tracks."

If you are not a citizen or previous citizen of Rockdale, maybe you can relate to this book. Maybe you lived across the tracks in your town, or maybe you know someone that does. Wherever you grew up, do all you can to build and repair the old wastes.

In most large cities there was or is a small shopping center consisting of food market, barber shop, beauty shops, (as my mother would say) what-not shop, and a gas station all in that neighborhood. This seems like a replica of the 50's with Pinkys, Bells, Franklin's Barber, Gray's Beauty, Ledbetters, etc. God has given me a vision since 1989 and I still have it written with plans in place. I was given 1 Samuel 30:8 as marching orders. My command is to pursue, overtake and recover all! The land has already been donated. God's plan will never fail.

Due to the help of private foundations and grants, AAOCC has been able to empower 104 or more pastors and caregivers each year with scholarships, books, and classes each year to give back to their communities. I challenge you to get involved, find resources and do all you can to improve the community, your communities.

About the Author:
##########

Dr. Dennis L. Brooks Sr. graduated from the American School of Marketing in San Francisco, CA. He attended New Mexico University, majoring in Sociology and Physical Education. He was employed with Western Electric Company/Lucent Technology from 1965 – 1985. He also attended ElCentro College, majoring in mid-Management. Dr. Brooks accepted the call to ministry in 1978 at New Hope Missionary Baptist Church, where he was licensed and ordained. He pastored at Springfield Missionary Baptist Church in Rockdale, from 1980 to 1985. Dr. Brooks received his Bachelor of Theology/Master of Divinity from Gospel Ministry Theological Institute in Houston, Texas. He also received a Bachelor of Biblical Studies, Master of Theology, Doctor of Ministry; a PhD in Pastoral Care and Clinical Counseling from Minnesota Graduate School of Theology, Supervising Clinical Therapist from American Academy of Clinical Family Therapist, PhD in Apostle of Ministry from the College of Apolistic Ministry, San Antonio Theological Seminary, and an Honorary Doctor of Divinity, from Christian Bible College. Dr. Brooks is the senior pastor and founder of New Jerusalem Interdenominational Church, the founder and President of the Institute for Teaching God's Word Theological Seminary, the American Academy of Crisis Counseling.

Dr. Brooks, and his wife, Clara Brooks, have hosted "Crisis Counseling" Workshops in many cities and states throughout the North America, and established schools with ministries from the American Samoa Islands, have traveled to Brussels Belgium, Germany and Paris France to establish schools and curriculum for Ministers from the Congo, as well as establishing a Bible school on the Island of Dominica.

My blessings: married 53 years, we have four grown sons, 13 grandchildren and five great-grandchildren. All of my sons were blessed with football scholarships, attending Angelo State, Howard Payne University, Texas Christian University, and Texas Tech University furthering careers with the Chicago Bears and Shreveport Pirates (Canadian Football League). I am proud of my boys for many reasons. Between the four of them, they have shown success as athletes with achievements of High School All-American, one college All-American, winning in the State, seven gold medals, six silver medals, two bronze medals, with two achieving school history to reach a 13 sub in 110 huddles. One son continues to hold the record for 300 huddles with a time of 36:3, since 1985 until present. I am honored to be blessed with a dynamic family. I have done my best to give my sons good roots. I am grateful!

My wife is a dynamic teacher in the ministry. She holds a doctorate degree and a certificate holder from Rhema Bible School. We still actively work together in the ministry. The name for the church came from her. She named the church New Jerusalem. She is a co-developer in all that we do. She has also helped to develop the curriculum and all the writings for lab, case studies, and field ministry. Together, we have traveled as far as Three Hills Alberta, Canada in order to receive knowledge and get the Institute for teaching God's Word started. I have to acknowledge her for being a part of the vision. All in Jesus' name.

Across the Tracks

Dennis L. Brooks, Sr. PhD

www.ingramcontent.com/pod-product-compliance
Lightning Source LLC
Chambersburg PA
CBHW070133100426
42744CB00009B/1814